Burkley and the Beasts:

The Sea Serpent

By Tiffany Nicole Smith

ISBN-13: 978-1507596944

About DyslexiAssist™

Part of our mission at Knowonder! Publishing is to make literacy more effective. In order to fulfill that mission for children suffering from dyslexia we are proud to announce our new DyslexiAssist™ initiative: to publish each of our books in a special font designed to make reading easier for dyslexics. You can learn more about it on our website at:

www.knowonder.com/dyslexiassist

When reading with this new font, independent research shows that 84% of dyslexics read faster, 77% read with fewer mistakes, and 76% recommend the font to others who suffer from dyslexia.

Reading stories is a highly enjoyable form of entertainment and learning for many people but people with dyslexia have been unable to find joy from books. We hope this new initiative can now bring the same love and joy of reading to your home!

I would like to express my gratitude to the people who saw me through this book:

To all members of the Smith and Lowe families— thank you for all your never-ending support and encouragement.

To Kathy Rygg, my fantastic editor— I greatly appreciate your advice and honest feedback. I'd like to thank you and everyone at Knowonder! Publishing for believing in Burkley.

To all the students I've taught throughout the years— your creativity and big imaginations make writing stories so fun and rewarding.

For my parents,

Vincent and Mary Smith

Table of Contents

1

Crewel Jewel
Strikes Again

"Burkley-Burkley-Burkley-Burk

Burk-Burk-Burk-Burk-Burk.

Burkley-Burkley-Burkley-Burk

Burk-Burk-Burk-Burk-Burk."

That was me singing a song I'd made up to the tune of "Old MacDonald".

"Burkley Brooks, control yourself!" That was Ms. Cooper.

"'Burkley, Burkley, Burkley' is my theme song. It helps me concentrate," I told her.

"That's nice, Burkley, but the rest of us can't concentrate with you singing."

"Sorry," I muttered.

Ms. Cooper sighed. "Students, you have fifteen minutes left to work on your projects."

Ms. Cooper was my third grade teacher at Fairfield Academy. My name is Burkley Brooks, but my family and friends call me Quirky Burkley because I do things differently from most people.

In science, we were working together to build a terrarium. That's a glass container where plants are grown. This was kind of a happy-sad situation. The happy part was that I was working with my BFF for always and eternity, Cheyenne. The sad part was that I was also working with Cruel Jewel, the meanest girl in the world. Nobody called her Cruel Jewel except for Cheyenne and me, but don't tell her that. She was being her usual bossy self, and Cheyenne and I didn't appreciate it.

"You two put in the soil. I can't get dirt in my nails," Jewel said, showing us her pink glittery nail polish.

"We're all going to put in the soil," Cheyenne said.

Jewel crossed her arms over her chest, giving us major attitude. "I'm not."

"You will or I'll bring my boa constrictor to school tomorrow and he'll swallow you whole!" I said, but I may have shouted it accidentally.

"Burkley Brooks, control yourself," Ms. Cooper said again.

"Yes, Ms. Cooper," I said, and Jewel laughed.

She did help us fill the container with soil

because she knows I really do have a boa constrictor named Stella.

Next, we had to stick in the grass seeds. Jewel looked like she was about to say she didn't want to do that either when I gave her my don't-even-try-it-look. She stuck her glittery-pink polished finger in that soil just like Cheyenne and me. Then Jewel wanted to be the only one who watered the seeds because that was the most important job.

I shook my head. "No, no, no. I will water one-third, Cheyenne will water one-third, and you can water one-third." I am very good with fractions.

Jewel insisted on going first. She took the watering can and poured water into the terrarium, but she didn't stop after her one-third. She was trying to water the whole thing. I grabbed the watering can from her, but she wouldn't let go. I pulled it toward me and she pulled it back toward her.

"Let go!" Jewel shouted.

So I did. Jewel fell back in her seat and water spilled everywhere.

"Look what you did, Broccoli!" Jewel shrieked. That's what she always called me—the grossest, stinkiest vegetable that ever existed. I told you she was mean.

The whole class stopped and stared at us. Ms. Cooper had on her "Oh-no-they-didn't" look. Then

Jewel began to cry like this wasn't all her fault,

but Ms. Cooper didn't buy it.

"Both of you, get paper towels and clean up

that mess," Ms. Cooper ordered. Then she said that

only Cheyenne could water the terrarium because

Jewel and I couldn't handle the responsibility. The

two of us grumbled as we sopped up the water with

balled-up paper towels.

After that came the paper part of our science

activity. We had to list the steps we took to

create our terrarium and draw a picture of it.

I used my best handwriting and only made one

mistake. I had meant to write "put" but I wrote

"pit". I couldn't erase it because I always made my

"i"s look like people. If I erased them, they wouldn't exist anymore and that's just mean. I circled the word "pit" and wrote, "Sorry, Ms. Cooper." Then I wrote the correct word next to it and included a smiley face and a special message. Today I wrote, "Ms. Cooper. I like your shoes."

I drew the most beautiful picture of a terrarium anyone had ever seen. I made the darkest, dirtiest soil and the greenest, lushest grass. It was spectacular! My drawing looked exactly like the actual terrarium. I looked back and forth at my picture and the terrarium, comparing the two. Suddenly something moved underneath the soil. I rubbed my eyes and looked some more. The soil moved again.

"Cheyenne, did you see that?" I whispered.

"See what?"

"The soil moved. There's something in it."

Cheyenne scrunched her face. "Ewww! Maybe it's a worm."

If it was a worm, we had to get it out of there. I stood over the terrarium and poked my pencil in the soil. It moved again, but this time something came out of it. At first I thought it was a worm—it looked long and slimy. But I've never seen a worm that big before. And I'm pretty sure they aren't usually green. The tentacle thing wagged at me and then disappeared underneath the soil.

"Did you guys see that?" I asked Cheyenne and Jewel.

Jewel rolled her eyes. "See what? You making holes in the soil?"

"No, a big slimy creature." I looked at the soil again. It didn't move anymore.

"Yeah right, Broccoli. You think there's an octopus in there?" Jewel asked.

I glanced at Cheyenne. The look on her face told me she didn't believe me either. I checked the terrarium again but still nothing. Maybe my eyes were playing tricks on me. Sometimes that can happen when you stare at something too long.

At the end of the day, Ms. Cooper handed our

science papers back, and she had made a major mistake on mine. There was a huge red zero at the top of my paper.

I went up to her desk. "Ms. Cooper, I think you forgot to write a 'one' and a 'zero' in front of this other 'zero'."

Jewel came up and her paper had a zero on it too.

"No, I didn't," Ms. Cooper said. "The grade for this science activity was based on how well you work together. That's why you both got a zero. Try harder next time."

The bell rang, and I shoved my paper down to the bottom of my backpack before anyone else could see it.

On the way to the bus I told Cheyenne how I was starting a collection of things shaped like circles. So far I had a nickel, a toy donut, a ponytail holder, and a wheel that had fallen off my cousin Hayden's toy car.

"Everybody knows you need more than four things for it to be called a collection," Jewel said from behind us, butting into my business.

"How about I rip that zero off your science paper and add it to my collection?" I was very proud of myself for coming up with that one until Jewel pointed out that a zero was actually an oval, not a circle. Touché, Jewel, touché. She also reminded me that I had gotten a zero on my science

paper too.

Double touché.

2

Quirky Burkley

When the bus dropped us off, I said goodbye to

Cheyenne even though I would probably see her

later. We're lucky because we live in townhomes

and our houses are actually stuck together.

My little sister, McKenna, was already home with Grandma Brooks. My grandma isn't a normal grandma. She's the coolest grandma ever. She actually rides a motorcycle with a group called Motor Divas. Grandma gets together with a few of her friends and they go for short trips on Sundays. How many grandmas do that? She even has a leopard-print helmet.

McKenna is only in half-day kindergarten so she gets out earlier than me. She was sitting at the table eating a peanut butter and banana sandwich (gross). McKenna reached for me with sticky fingers, begging for a hug. I ignored her.

"Don't be rude," Grandma said. "Hug your sister."

"But she's all dirty," I whined. I hugged her anyway and sure enough, she got peanut butter all over the back of my shirt.

I went to the refrigerator for a snack. I don't let Grandma make snacks for me. I'm old enough to make my own. I knocked on the fridge before opening the door to warn the food. My family thinks it's silly, but I think it's only polite. I like food and I don't want to disturb it. My parents expect us to knock on their door before coming in, so why should it be any different for the food?

I chose a bag of apple slices and a cheese stick. When I was done with my snack, I made sure to leave a bite of an apple slice and a tiny piece of cheese for my invisible friend Guadalupe. Guadalupe is an itty-bitty fairy so she doesn't eat much. I always leave her a tiny bit of whatever I eat.

"Your parents are coming home early today and we're going out to eat, so get your homework done," Grandma said.

I waved my hands in the air and hopped on one foot. That was my happy dance. My mom and dad are both nurses and work crazy hours. Some days I don't even see them at all. Going out to eat is one of my favorite things to do.

I hurried to get my homework done and then I changed from my school uniform to my favorite outfit—a purple tank top, pink tutu skirt, my leopard-print high top sneakers with pink laces, yellow tights, and my special ring. My special ring has a purple heart-shaped stone that Cheyenne had given me as a friendship ring.

That night we went to Dad's favorite seafood place, the Lobster House. I don't care much for seafood, but it was Daddy's turn to pick the restaurant. The waitress came to the table and handed us menus. She gave McKenna and me each a children's menu with a box of crayons that only had four colors—red, yellow, blue, and green. I don't care for restaurant crayons because they never have

pink or purple—the best colors ever.

"I'd like a grown-up menu, please," I told the

waitress.

Mom shook her head. "No, Burkley. You're not

going to like anything on it and it's going to be a

waste of food and money."

"It won't be a waste. I promise."

Mom looked at Daddy and he nodded. It was

always easier to get a yes from him than from

Mommy. The waitress gave me a grown-up menu and

I decided to order something exotic and different

that I had never tried before.

When the waitress came back she took everyone's order. McKenna ordered some boring old fish sticks that she could have anytime. Me on the other hand, I ordered the Ultimate Feast, which came with calamari (that's squid), crab legs, and lobster tail.

"Excuse me, but there can't be anything yellow on my plate and there has to be something red," I told the waitress.

My P.E. teacher always says, "You are what you eat." So I have to be very careful with what I put in my body. Red is a warm fiery color—the color of courage, so I like to eat red things. They make me feel brave and toasty inside. Although yellow can be a very nice color, I don't want to eat it.

Once on TV I heard a man call someone a yellow-

bellied chicken. When I asked Daddy what that

meant, he told me the man was calling the other

one a coward. I want to be brave, so nothing yellow

for me.

The waitress smiled at me. "Okay, the shell of

your lobster tail will be red and I won't bring you

any lemon or butter."

When the waitress brought our food I

immediately regretted my decision. My food looked

absolutely disgusting. The crab legs looked like real

crab legs. I had to crack them open myself! The

lobster tail didn't look like anything anybody should

eat. But the worst was the calamari. It looked like cut up parts of an octopus monster. I've had calamari before and it kind of looked like onion rings. This calamari looked like it had just been pulled from the ocean. Everybody watched, waiting for me to dig in. It was too late to turn back now.

I watched McKenna as she happily dipped her fish sticks into the tartar sauce, and I wished I had ordered something boring like her. I had promised I would eat all my food, so I had to at least try. I dug my fork into the soft meat of the lobster tail. It wasn't so bad. Daddy cracked open the crab legs for me. I picked the meat out and it was pretty good too.

"Try that octopus stuff," McKenna said.

I narrowed my eyes at her. "It's not octopus." Now that she had brought attention to it, everyone was watching. "Um, I want to save it for Guadalupe."

Daddy frowned. "I thought Guadalupe was allergic to seafood."

He was right. Seafood made her break out in hives. I took a deep breath. Maybe if I pinched my nose it wouldn't be so bad. When I tried to stick my fork into one of the calamari tentacles, a tiny snake's tail came out from underneath it. The tail had green and brown scales. My eyes had to be playing tricks on me like in science class. I closed

my eyes and shook my head. When I opened them

again, the snake tail was still there swinging back

and forth. I looked at my family. They were eating

and didn't notice.

"Did you guys see that?" I asked.

"See what, honey?" Dad asked.

"A snake's tail. It just came out of my

calamari."

Everyone stared at me like I had three heads.

"It did. Look!" I pushed the squid away with my

fork so they could see the snake's tail, but nothing

was there.

"Stop playing around," Mom said. "If you don't want to eat it, you don't have to, but don't be dramatic."

"I'm not being dramatic!" I shouted.

"We are in a restaurant. Lower your voice," Mom ordered.

"Is Burkley going to get punished for yelling?" McKenna asked.

"You be quiet or I'll tell Stella to swallow you whole!" I shouted, and McKenna started to cry because she's afraid of Stella. She wailed across the whole restaurant and everyone stared at us.

Then Mom got fed up and we had to leave

because McKenna had ruined dinner. You just can't

take little kids anywhere.

3

Grandpa Brooks and
Uncle Charlie

The next morning I ate my special breakfast—a

bowl of Chocolate Os with a glass of milk. I don't

like my milk and cereal mixed together like everyone

else. I always eat my cereal by itself and then I

drink my milk.

"Why so glum this morning?" Grandma asked after she kissed me on the forehead. Mom and Dad had already left for work. McKenna was also eating Chocolate Os while she read the back of the cereal box.

"Nobody believed me last night," I answered. "But I wasn't lying, Grandma.

There was something alive in my food."

"I believe you," Grandma said quietly.

"You do? Why?"

Grandma sat at the kitchen table in front of me. McKenna was still reading, not paying us any attention.

"Burkley," Grandma said. "I think you're at the age now."

"At the age of what?"

"Where you're old enough to get the vision," Grandma answered.

"What vision?" I asked.

"Yeah, what vision?" asked McKenna, who apparently was listening.

"The same ones your grandpa and Uncle Charlie used to have—when you see things nobody else can."

"But why? Why am I seeing these things?"

Grandma put a juice pouch and a package of crackers in McKenna's backpack. "You're special. You have a gift."

McKenna scowled. "So, I'm not special?"

"Of course you are, sweetheart. You're special in a different way, that's all."

McKenna smiled and I stood a little taller. I liked being special. "Tell me more, Grandma."

"It's time for school," Grandma said. "I'll explain it all to you later."

I knew I would spend the entire school day wondering what Grandma meant. Was it something good or bad? Why was I special?

"Boys and girls, it's almost science fair time," Ms. Cooper announced that morning at school. "The science fair will be held in two weeks, so today I'm going to pair you up with a partner."

I looked at the other kids sitting in my group. Everyone looked worried. No one wanted to be paired up with Martin, Jewel, Humphrey, or Oliver. Martin never did his work. Humphrey always smelled like old lima beans, and one time Oliver ate a cricket. Boys are vile.

As Ms. Cooper called out the names for partners, I prayed and crossed my fingers.

"Burkley Brooks and Jewel McDonald," I heard

Ms. Cooper say. Grasshoppers!

It was bad enough I had to sit across from her every day, now I would have to work on a project with her for two weeks. Ms. Cooper must have been punishing us for the terrarium mess from yesterday. As if giving us both zeroes wasn't bad enough.

Jewel gave me a mean look. "Don't think I'm going to be doing all the work just because I'm smarter than you at everything. And we better win first place!"

"I'm going to make the best science project in the history of science projects! You better be able to keep up with my science-geniusness," I told her.

"If you were really a genius, you would know geniusness is not a real word, Broccoli."

This was going to be the longest two weeks of my life.

That day my cousin Hayden was spending the night. Grandma watches him when his mother has to work late at the airport. Aunt Michelle is a gate attendant. She takes the boarding passes from people before they get on the plane.

"Did you feed him this week?" Hayden asked, staring at Stella in his glass tank. Stella is the most beautiful boa constrictor in the world. He has brown skin with a pattern that looks like black rhombuses. When I got him, my cousin Hayden told me Stella was a girl's name and my boa constrictor was a boy. I told him Stella was my boa and I would name him whatever I wanted.

"No, not yet. Tomorrow I have to go to the pet store and get a rat," I answered.

"Aww," Hayden groaned. He always liked to help me feed Stella.

Most girls I know think it's gross to have a pet snake and even worse to feed it rats, but Daddy says it's nature. Stella has to eat just like we do. My parents bought Stella for me last Christmas. Mom hates snakes, but she let me have Stella as long as I keep him in my room and make sure he

never escapes from his tank. Stella has gotten out

once. I found him curled up in the bathtub, but I

didn't tell Mom about that.

At bedtime, Grandma tucked us in. When

Hayden spends the night, he sleeps in a sleeping

bag on my floor. McKenna climbed into the top bunk

while I pulled the cover over me on the bottom

bunk.

"Grandma, what about the vision?" I asked. I'd

been thinking about it all day.

I sat up and Grandma sat on my bed with me.

McKenna crawled back down to join us, and Hayden

listened from his sleeping bag.

"Remember how I've always told you children that your Grandpa Brooks was the first African American to be inducted into the Explorer's Hall of Fame?" Grandma asked.

We remembered. Grandma always told us stories about our grandfather, the great explorer. Unfortunately, he and their son, our Uncle Charlie, had disappeared during an exploration before we were even born.

"There's a way to save them. I've tried before, but I'm only a Brooks by marriage, not by blood. I can't be the one to save them." Grandma said.

"Grandma, what are you talking about?" Hayden asked.

She dug into the pocket of her robe and took out a beautiful heart-shaped locket on a gold chain. The heart was a pink stone. It reminded me of the heart in my friendship ring, but the stone in this heart was real. It looked very expensive.

"What's that?" McKenna asked, grabbing the necklace. She had to touch everything.

"This is the Heartstone. It's the key to the portal," Grandma answered.

"Portal?" the three of us asked at the same time.

"Yes. It's where your uncle and grandfather disappeared. It's a special place in the world where your grandfather went to study mythical creatures so he could bring back information. But something went wrong and Grandpa got trapped. Your Uncle Charlie was trying to bring him back by putting a puzzle together. See, each time Uncle Charlie defeated a monster he would earn a puzzle piece. Once the puzzle was completely put together, Uncle Charlie would have been able to see where your Grandpa was so he could bring him back. Charlie was able to collect eight pieces. There are probably a dozen more."

"Grandma?" McKenna asked. "Is this a true

story or make-believe?"

"Oh, it's absolutely true, sweetheart," Grandma said. "And I will have to tell you the rest later because it is past your bedtime. Good night."

I went to sleep not wanting to believe Grandma, but I thought about the snake's tongue I had seen in the terrarium and then the tail at the restaurant. Maybe my eyes weren't playing tricks on me after all. Maybe I had perfect vision!

4

SCIENCE PROJECT, SCHMIENCE PROJECT

"We are going to be doing our science project

on acid rain," Jewel told me. Ms. Cooper had given

us time to work on our science projects with our

partners. Jewel, as usual, was being Ms. Bossy-

pants.

"No," I said. Grandma told me you should never

let anyone boss you around, except your parents

and teachers. "I want to do something on the

ocean." Ever since Hayden and I watched a TV

show about dolphins, I'd been interested in sea life.

Oceans are cool.

"Well, I want to do acid rain."

"Why don't you take a vote?" asked a kid

named Devin who sat beside us.

"What good would that do? There's only two of

us. It would just be a tie, dummy," Jewel said.

"Don't call him a dummy," I told her. "He was only trying to help. Why don't we do Rock, Paper, Scissors?"

"But—" Jewel began.

I got my hand ready. "One, two, three."

Reluctantly, Jewel put her hand out.

"Rock, paper, scissors, shoot!" I held my hand out flat like a piece of paper. Jewel chose the rock by keeping her fist closed. Everybody knows that paper beats rock, so I won. "Sorry, Jewel," I said.

Jewel folded her arms across her chest and wouldn't say anything to me. Cheyenne and her science partner Max were sitting across from us.

Max was drawing a picture of a zombie, which had nothing to do with their project. Cheyenne would probably end up doing all the work, but I would still rather work with Max than with Jewel.

"Jewel, I know you're upset, but this is going to be really fun. I thought the title of our project could be 'All About Jellyfish'."

"How about 'All About pffff?'" Jewel said, sticking out her tongue and spitting at me. Really? McKenna does that when she's mad, but she's five.

"You want to come to my house and work on it one day after school?" I asked.

"No way. I'm not stepping foot in your house

with that monster!" Jewel cried.

"Stella is not a monster. He's a reptile and he behaves better than you," I said.

"Whatever, Broccoli. We'll work at my house. I have dance class today, so we'll meet tomorrow."

I didn't really want to go to her house, but I'd gotten my way with the science fair project, so I didn't have much choice.

"I'm going to pull all my hair out before this science fair is over. Max is so lazy." Cheyenne shook her head as she sat next to me on the bus.

"Tell me about it," I moaned.

"I wrote down some notes for our project on a piece of paper and Max fell asleep and drooled on it. I'd never seen one person make so much drool before," Cheyenne said.

"I'd rather work with a drooler than with Cruel Jewel. She was so mean to me the whole time. The worst part is that I have to go to her house. Her house!"

Cheyenne shook her head. "That's terrible. It's going to be a long two weeks for both of us."

Mom was home. I was happy to see her at first, but then I wasn't happy because she made me do the dishes. McKenna was coloring at the kitchen table and Hayden was getting a head start on his homework, which wasn't fair. He was going to finish before me and go outside to play, leaving me inside working on math problems.

I filled the sink with suds and started washing the dishes. I washed the glasses first like Mom had showed me. Three were done when I reached down to see if there were any more. I felt something weird and yanked my hand back out of the water. Something slimy had wrapped around my hand, kind of like Stella, but I knew he wasn't in the sink. I stuck my hand back in and felt the thing tighten around my fingers. I got my hand out and drained the water to see what was going on. After the water was gone, there were still suds at the bottom of the sink, and something moved underneath them!

I blew the bubbles out of the way and noticed a long slimy thing sticking out of the drain. It was another snake's tail—green and brown, waving back and forth at me. It was just like the one I had seen in the restaurant, except it was much larger.

"Hayden, look!" I shouted.

"What?" he asked.

"Look! Come quick!"

"No, you just don't want to do the dishes," he said.

The snake's tail whipped around, knocking over a glass sitting in the sink. It didn't break, but it made a loud clinking sound.

Mom ran into the kitchen. "Did something break?"

"It wasn't me, Mom. It was the snake's tail."

Mom frowned at me. "What have I told you about fibbing?"

"But I'm not fibbing. Look!" Just as I said that, the snake's tail slithered down the drain.

I looked back and Grandma was standing in the doorway of the kitchen. She nodded, and I knew it was time to find out more about the portal.

5

THE HEARTSTONE

Grandma helped me with the rest of the dishes.

Then she finished telling McKenna, Hayden, and me

the story of the special stone.

We curled up next to her on her bed and she

opened up a photo album. There were pictures of my

grandpa and Uncle Charlie holding up giant fish they

had caught and pictures of them in cool-looking

places—like the white shores of the Galapagos Islands and the sharp peaks of the Andes Mountains—places I had never seen. I'd always felt sorry for Grandma because her husband and son were missing. I felt sorry for my dad because he didn't know where his dad and brother were. I also felt sorry for myself because I never knew my grandfather and uncle. They had been gone for ten years. Grandma had told us the story of how they disappeared plenty of times, but I'd always felt like she was leaving something out.

"Your grandpa was inspired by his father to be a great explorer. Great-grandpa Brooks always told Grandpa stories about magical places and mythical creatures. Your grandpa's father had always wanted to go to a place called Mermaid's Lagoon, but he never made it. He became too sick to continue going on explorations. Grandpa was determined to get there to fulfill his father's dream. I tried to tell him many times there was probably no such place as Mermaid's Lagoon, but Grandpa was determined."

A tear rolled down Grandma's cheek. I wiped it away with my finger.

"His father told him where to go to find an Italian man who would give him instructions on how to reach Mermaid's Lagoon. Your grandpa bought a boat, which he named the **S.S. Brooks.**" Grandma stroked the Heartstone in her hand. "He told me he had found the gentleman who was selling this locket in a tiny Italian village. The old man said it was a key to a magical land filled with rare, exotic creatures—just like Great-grandpa had said. Grandpa was so excited to have finally found the key, he bought the Heartstone from the man. Your grandfather thought he could find the Plesiosaurus, which everyone had thought to be extinct."

"A plesio what?" McKenna asked.

"A Plesiosaurus. It's a reptile that lived in the ocean during the early part of the Jurassic Period—you know, the times of the dinosaurs. It's a large creature with a small head, a long slender neck, a wide body like a turtle, and a short tail. It also has two arms that are like large paddles."

"Did he find it?" Hayden asked.

Grandma closed the photo album. "I don't know. When I last spoke to him by phone, your grandfather told me he was stopping at an inn for the night. He had plans of traveling to Mermaid's Lagoon the next day, but a terrible storm was brewing. That was the last I heard from him. Weeks later, I received a letter from someone. I found this locket with the heart-shaped stone at the bottom of the envelope. It was from Menorah, The Sea Queen of Mermaid's Lagoon."

I took the locket in my hand. "She sent you

Grandpa's Heartstone. What did the letter say, Grandma?"

"Menorah wrote that her sister Sedna, the other Sea Queen, was holding your grandpa hostage for trespassing in her territory. Sedna and Menorah are twin sisters who rule Mermaid's Lagoon together. Menorah is a very kind and fair queen, but her sister is just plain evil. Do you children know what a compromise is?"

We shook our heads.

"A compromise is when people don't quite agree on something, they both give in a little so each person can have some of what they want. Menorah wanted to set Grandpa free, but Sedna wanted to

keep him as a prisoner forever, so the sisters

compromised. Sedna agreed to free Grandpa, but

only if someone in our family completed a series of

tasks. See, little ones, not everyone believes in

other worlds and creatures that we've never seen,

but your grandfather and Uncle Charlie always

have. I tried to go to Mermaid's Lagoon to help

Grandpa, but the Heartstone didn't work for me. I

realized for a person to go through the portal, they

had to be a Brooks by blood. "

"So what did you do, Grandma?" McKenna

asked.

"That only left your Uncle Charlie and your

father. Girls, your father was never one who believed in magical things, not even when he was a little boy. A person who doesn't believe can't go through the portal. Uncle Charlie was the only candidate. I didn't want him to go. Who knew how dangerous it would be? But sending him was the only way our family would be whole again. So Uncle Charlie began the mission. At first, everything went well. After each task, he earned a puzzle piece from Queen Menorah. The completed puzzle would reveal Grandpa's location. Uncle Charlie earned eight pieces, but the last time he went through the portal, he didn't come back. I should never have let him go."

"It's not your fault, Grandma," Hayden said.

"It's that awful Queen Sedna."

"Where are the puzzle pieces, Grandma?"
McKenna asked.

"Hayden, pass me the envelope in that top
drawer," Grandma said.

Hayden opened the drawer, pulled out a large
yellow envelope, and handed it to Grandma. She
turned it upside-down and eight black pieces fell
onto the bedspread.

"But these pieces are blank, Grandma. How can
you tell what the picture's supposed to be?" I
asked.

"They will stay blacked out until all the pieces have been collected. Then they will reveal the location," Grandma explained.

"So, why have I been seeing these weird things?"

"Because, Burkley, you have the sight."

"Why me?"

"Right after you were born, I received a letter in the mail. Wrapped in the letter was the Heartstone your grandpa and Uncle Charlie had worn to go to Mermaid's Lagoon. The letter stated as the next oldest Brooks, you were in line to take their place."

"Aww," Hayden whined. "Why Burkley and not me? We're the same age."

"Probably because she's four months older," Grandma answered. It was true. I liked to tease him about being older, but right then I wished he was the oldest. Hayden seemed to want the job, but I was terrified.

"Burkley, you're the key to the portal now," Grandma said.

"What does that mean?" Hayden asked.

"It means Burkley has to wear the stone around her neck to be able to go through the portal. Once she goes through, she'll meet a man named Gaston.

Your Uncle Charlie would tell me about him whenever he came back from a challenge. Gaston will tell her the goal for the task as well as give her a weapon."

"Weapon?" I asked.

Grandma nodded. "Yes. It may be a lightning sword or a bow and arrow. Something that will help you defeat the creature you have to face."

"Creature?" McKenna squeaked. She looked petrified. I was too on the inside, but I didn't show it.

"Yes. That's how Burkley will earn the puzzle pieces. She has to defeat the creatures."

"That sounds crazy," Hayden said.

Grandma patted his head. "I know, sweetheart, but it's true. Your uncle has been through the portal. He's defeated creatures. How do you think I got these puzzle pieces?"

"How do you know when it's time to go?" I asked.

"When you start seeing strange things, that's when it's time to go through the portal."

I shook my head. "B-but I have to do a science project. I can't go through any portals right now."

Grandma laughed. "No, honey, it doesn't work like that. When you go through the portal, time here doesn't pass when you're gone. That means if you leave at five o'clock, when you get back it'll still be five o'clock."

McKenna rested her head against Grandma's arm. "What's on the other side of the portal, Grandma?"

"Mermaid's Lagoon, where your grandpa was trying to go. Queen Menorah sent a letter with instructions for how to get there. It said you must stand in the back of your closet wearing the Heartstone."

"What kinds of things did Uncle Charlie fight?" Hayden asked.

Grandma looked at the ceiling. "Let's see, he told me about a giant octopus, an evil mermaid, a creature made of sea weed, and a few other minor things."

I had a feeling those minor things weren't so minor. "I can't beat any creatures, Grandma."

"Yes you can, my love. You wouldn't be seeing the creatures if you weren't equipped to fight them."

"I have to go by myself?" I asked.

"I'm not sure. Your Uncle Charlie went alone. You can try to take someone else in the portal with you and see what happens."

"Cool!" Hayden shouted. "I'll go with you. Don't worry, Burk. I can beat any of those creatures."

"Not me," McKenna said, shaking her head. "I don't want to go."

"You don't have to go if you don't want to, McKenna," Grandma said. "Burkley decides when to go, but you have to go soon. Queen Menorah is summoning you."

6

TALL TALES

"Do you really expect me to believe that?"

Cheyenne asked as she bit into half of my peanut

butter and jelly sandwich. We always do that. I

give her half of my peanut butter and jelly sandwich

and she gives me half of her turkey and Swiss

cheese.

"You think I'm lying?" I asked.

"Yep," Cheyenne answered.

"When have I ever lied to you?"

Cheyenne thought for a second. "Let's see,

there was the time you told me you saw a monkey

outside your window. Last year you told me you

were moving to the North Pole to live with Santa

because your mom wouldn't let you stay up late.

You told me that McKenna had been abducted by

aliens, but they sent her back because she was so

annoying. Just last week—"

"Okay!"

"Why should I believe you now?" Cheyenne asked.

"Because I'm telling you the truth right now. You can ask my grandma. I can show you the Heartstone and the puzzle pieces."

Cheyenne narrowed her eyes then pointed her spoon at me. She made beeping noises while making circular motions with the spoon.

"Umm...Cheyenne, what are you doing?"

"This is a lie detector. I'm trying to see if you're lying." She beeped for ten more seconds. "Okay, no lies found. I believe you." Her green eyes grew wide. "Wow, Burkley. How cool is that? You get to go through a portal and battle creatures. That sounds like a movie or something."

"The best part is that you can come, too."

Her smile dropped. "Oh, great."

"What's wrong?" I switched her red apple for my yellow pear. Now that I was going through some portal to face dangerous creatures, I wanted to eat as many red foods as possible. I needed all the courage I could get.

"I don't know about that. It sounds awfully dangerous," she said, biting into the pear.

"I know, but it'll be okay. Hayden's going too. I

think the more people we have the better."

Cheyenne shook her head. "Burkley, I can't. I'm...scared."

"I know. I'm scared too. But we'll be together. Please, Cheyenne, I'd do it for you."

She thought about it for a few seconds. "Okay, but only because you're my BFF for always and eternity."

After I had finished my homework that afternoon, Grandma walked me to Cruel Jewel's house. Jewel lived two blocks away and that was way too close. I rang the doorbell and waited. A lady who looked just like Jewel answered the door.

She smiled at us.

"Umm, good afternoon, Mrs. Jewel's Mom. I'm Burkley Brooks and this is my grandma."

"Of course," Mrs. Jewel's Mom said, shaking my grandma's hand. "It's so nice to meet you."

"Likewise," Grandma said. "Burkley, I'll be back in an hour. Mind your manners."

"Okay, Grandma." I watched her walk back down the porch to the sidewalk. I was stuck with Jewel for the next sixty minutes—sixty loooong minutes.

Mrs. Jewel's Mom led me inside, and I had the urge to tell her how horrible, mean, and rude her daughter was, but I didn't. She lived with Jewel, so I figured she already knew.

"Jewel is upstairs in her room, and you can call me Nancy," she said. I would call her Ms. Nancy because Grandma said I shouldn't call adults by their first names. Ms. Nancy walked me to Jewel's room. "Jewel, your friend is here."

"She is not my friend."

"Jewel," her mother warned. "Be nice. I'll bring you girls a snack in a few minutes."

I walked into the pinkest room I had ever seen. The walls were bubble gum pink. The comforter on her bed was watermelon pink. The carpet was cotton candy pink. Pink is my favorite color too, but this was over the top, just like Jewel.

She sat at her desk with a pink pen doing her homework in a pink notebook. I waited for her to say something, but she didn't.

"Well, we only have an hour so I guess we should get started," I said, sitting on her bed.

"Ewww!" she said, turning around. "Don't sit on my bed. I have to sleep there!"

So what? She was acting like I had cooties. "Then where should I sit?"

"On the floor," she answered.

That wasn't happening. I ignored her and pulled

a notebook from my backpack. "I made a list of

things we could include in our project about

jellyfish." I opened my notebook to the list. "What

they look like, what they eat, their habitat—"

"Jellyfish are disgusting," Jewel said, rudely

interrupting me. "You would pick the most

disgusting creature in the ocean."

"Jellyfish are far from the most disgusting

creatures in the ocean, for your information. There's

the Viperfish. They have teeth so big they almost

go up to its eyes. It's one of the ugliest things I've

ever seen. Then there's the Blobfish. It looks like a

cartoon person with a gigantic nose. And then

there's the Vampire Squid that can hypnotize its

prey."

"There's no such thing. You're making that up,"

Jewel said.

"I am not. I saw it on the Discovery Channel."

Ms. Nancy came back into the room. "Here we

go, girls." She carried a tray—a tray filled with two

bananas, two bowls of applesauce, and diced

pineapples. Everything was yellow!

I gulped and said thank you because Grandma

had told me to mind my manners. I couldn't very

well tell the lady I didn't want any of her yellow-

bellied food. Maybe I could sneak the banana into

my backpack to give to Guadalupe later.

"Thanks, Mom," Jewel said, grabbing a banana and peeling it. "Well, aren't you going to eat something?" Jewel asked after her mother had left.

I shook my head.

"Why not?"

"I don't eat anything yellow."

"Why?" Jewel asked.

"I just don't." I wasn't going to waste my breath trying to explain it to her.

Jewel rolled her eyes. "You're a weird kid, Broccoli."

"Anyway, can I use your laptop to look up some stuff about jellyfish?" I asked.

"No, you may not. I'll look it up and you write down in your ugly notebook what I find."

I sighed and grabbed my pen. I looked at my purple watch. Fifty minutes left. Fifty loooong minutes.

I sat on Jewel's bed and waited patiently for her to pull up information on the jellyfish. I looked at the tray of yellow food sitting beside me. The applesauce began to move in the bowl. I looked at Jewel. She was focused on her laptop. Then a red snake's tongue came out of the applesauce and wrapped itself around the banana still sitting on the

tray. The tongue and the banana disappeared

underneath the applesauce. I grabbed a spoon from

the tray and stirred it. There was nothing there.

"Whoa!"

Jewel sighed. "I'm trying to concentrate here."

Then she looked at the tray. "I thought you said

you didn't eat yellow food."

"I don't."

"Then where's the banana?" Jewel asked.

"A snake's tongue came out of the applesauce

and took it."

Jewel stood and put her hands on her hips.

"What kind of fool do you take me for?"

"I'm telling the truth, Jewel. If I ate the

banana, where's the peel?"

Jewel rolled her eyes. "I think it's time for you

to go."

I decided then that I'd better get to Mermaid's

Lagoon ASAP.

"How was it?" Cheyenne asked after I got back

from Jewel's earlier than planned.

"Worse than I thought. She was mean the

whole time. She wouldn't let me use her laptop and

her mother served all yellow food. I saw another

snake's tongue too—in the applesauce. I told Jewel

but she didn't believe me. Instead she just kicked

me out. It was awful, Cheyenne."

"I'm glad you survived." Cheyenne hugged me.

We stood in front of Stella's tank watching him

digest a rat. I know it sounds mean, but as Dad

says, it's the circle of life. I wouldn't be able to

take Stella out of his tank to play with him for a

few days or he might throw up (now that would be

gross).

"Show it to me," Cheyenne said.

"What?"

"The Heartstone. I want to see it," Cheyenne

answered.

"Okay."

We went to Grandma's room and knocked on the door. She let us in.

"Grandma, I saw another snake's tongue at Jewel's house. It came out of the applesauce and stole my banana."

Grandma's eyes lit up. "It sounds like you'd better get to Mermaid's Lagoon sooner than later."

"You miss them a lot don't you, Grandma?"

Grandma nodded. "I do. I can't wait to see them again."

"Don't worry, Grandma. I plan on going today. Can we show Cheyenne the Heartstone?"

"Sure." Grandma went to her nightstand and pulled out the black velvet box. She opened it for Cheyenne to look inside.

Cheyenne gasped when she saw it. "It's beautiful."

"Turn around," Grandma said. I did and she fastened it around my neck.

I looked down at it. "I love it. Can you imagine the look on Jewel's face when she sees me wearing this?"

Grandma shook her head. "Oh no, Burkley. This

stone may never leave the house. If it's lost, we can never get through the portal again, and your uncle and grandfather will be lost forever."

Jewel was always bringing her new, pretty things to school and bragging about them. For once, I wanted to bring something cool. I was sure she had never had anything like this Heartstone.

Grandma put her hand on my shoulder. "Do you understand me, Burkley? This is very important."

"I understand."

Then Grandma handed me the black box covered in velvet and told me I was to keep the Heartstone in there at all times unless I was going through the portal.

Back in my room, I prepared myself for the first trip. I put on my favorite outfit—my purple tank top, pink tutu skirt, my leopard-print high tops with the pink shoelaces, my yellow tights, and my special friendship ring from Cheyenne. It matched the Heartstone, so it was perfect. We would leave as soon as Aunt Michelle brought Hayden over.

"Do you think it's really real, Burkley? Do you think we're really going to go somewhere?" Cheyenne asked.

"Of course I do. Grandma wouldn't lie to me."

"I'm coming too," McKenna said, putting on her

shoes.

"No, you're not. You told me yesterday you were too scared," I reminded her.

"I was just kidding." She always said that when she wanted to change her mind. "Can you tie my shoes?"

"Seriously? You think you can help us fight creatures when you can't even tie your own shoes?" I asked.

"I'm learning, okay? I'm only five. You just learned to tie your shoes last month!" McKenna yelled.

That is totally not true, by the way.

I sighed and tied her shoes in double knots for her, hoping she would change her mind. Little kids always have a way of messing things up.

Aunt Michelle finally dropped Hayden off.

"Maybe we should pack a basket full of food in case we get hungry," Hayden suggested. He was always thinking about food.

"Hayden, how are we supposed to battle creatures carrying a picnic basket? Lame-O! Have you ever seen a superhero carrying a picnic basket?" I asked.

"You know you're not a superhero, right?" Hayden went to pack a basket of food anyway.

"Maybe not now, but if I save Grandpa and Uncle Charlie I will be. Super Burkley to the rescue!"

"Umm, Burkley?" Cheyenne said. "Can we just get this over with before I change my mind?"

"Fine. We have to go through my closet," I said.

We went to Grandma's room where she was reading a book on her bed.

"We're ready, Grandma," I announced.

She closed her book and sat up. "Are you sure? Once you start your quest, you can't come back until you've earned a puzzle piece."

I wished she had told us this before. Maybe

packing a picnic basket was a good idea after all.

"You mean we can't come back when we want to?"

"That's right," Grandma said. "When Gaston

says you're done, that's when you're done."

Before, I had tried to be brave for the others,

but my stomach suddenly tied itself into double

knots like I had done with McKenna's shoelaces.

"But Grandma, what if we can't beat the creature?

What if it beats us? We'll never come back." I was

afraid of being trapped there like Grandpa and

Uncle Charlie.

Grandma put her hand on my cheek. "You're

Burkley Brooks. You can do anything you put your mind to."

"But—" I started to say. I still wasn't sure.

Grandma sat on her bed as Hayden came back with the picnic basket. "You don't have to do this, Burkley. But if you don't, Grandpa and Uncle Charlie will be lost forever."

I glanced at the others. They looked just as afraid as me, but they were willing to go.

"We've got to do this, Burkley. I've always wanted to meet Grandpa Brooks and Uncle Charlie," Hayden said.

I took a deep breath and touched the pink

Heartstone around my neck. "Okay, let's go."

We followed Grandma back to my bedroom and stood in front of the closet. Grandma opened the door for us. Hayden, Cheyenne, and I stepped inside. McKenna froze, her face turning a pale green color as if she had just eaten raw fish. "Uh, I don't think I'm going to go. Maybe next time."

Relieved, I took a deep breath. "Don't worry, Kenna. I'll tell you all about it when we get back."

"See you soon with that puzzle piece," Grandma said. Then she winked and closed the door.

"Bring me back a souvenir!" McKenna yelled through the door.

"Okay, guys," I said, holding my hands out. We formed a circle and closed our eyes. At first, nothing happened. Then there was a bright flash of light. I felt a cool burst of wind that caused me to shiver. The wind became so strong I fell backwards onto Hayden.

"Oww!" he moaned.

Before I could tell him I was sorry, cool water splashed over me, and I realized we were sliding downward. It was like the giant slide at the water park we went to last summer.

I put my hands up. "Woo-hoo!"

"Awesome!" Hayden yelled as we looped and

curved in the darkness.

Cheyenne was surprisingly quiet.

I slowed down and saw another flash of light.

Then everything fell silent.

7

THROUGH THE PORTAL

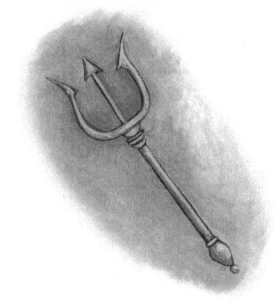

After the flash of bright light, everything turned

pitch black. Nobody spoke, and I was afraid to open

my eyes. I heard my heart pounding.

"Burkley," Cheyenne whispered.

I opened my eyes. The three of us were still

together, but we weren't in my closet anymore. We stood on the shore of an ocean. Wind whipped around us and waves crashed. My feet sank into the warm sand. I was standing in a place where my uncle and grandpa had been. It made me feel close to them.

Cheyenne looked like a shocked statue.

"Cheyenne, are you okay?" I asked.

Cheyenne nodded. "That...was...amazing!" She rubbed her eyes. "Is this really happening?"

"Yes," Hayden answered. "I knew Grandma was telling the truth."

Traveling through the portal to get to

Mermaid's Lagoon had been fun, but it was time to get down to business. "Now what are we supposed to do?" I asked.

"Look," Hayden said, pointing to a cave behind me.

I hadn't noticed the cave at first, but there was a purple light coming from it.

"Should we go in?" I asked.

"It beats standing out here wasting time," Hayden said.

He walked ahead, and Cheyenne and I followed him to the cave. I stopped when I saw something glisten in the yellow sand. I knelt for a closer look.

It was a beautiful gold coin. I picked it up. There were no symbols or pictures on either side of the coin.

"This is going in my circle collection." I slid the coin inside my high-top sneaker for safe-keeping.

"Come on, guys," Hayden said as he continued to walk. "I wonder if that coin is from a pirate treasure or something?"

It would be really cool if it was.

We reached the entrance of the cave and stood there for a second. I didn't want to admit I was afraid to go in.

"Y-you should go first," Cheyenne said to me.

"Why me?"

"You're wearing the Heartstone," Hayden said, suddenly sounding not-so-brave.

"All right, all right." I tiptoed forward, stopping at the mouth of the cave. I didn't want to go in at first, but then I thought about the people who were depending on me. If Grandpa and Uncle Charlie had done it, I could do it too.

"We'll wait out here," Cheyenne said.

"No way," I told her. "If I'm going in, everyone's going in."

It was still hard to see even though the cave was lit with a faint purple light. Holding hands, the three of us shuffled in until we heard something

move, then we stopped.

"What's that?" Cheyenne whispered.

"Don't worry," Hayden said. "Whatever it is,

I'll take care of it." But he didn't budge.

"Who's there?" shouted a voice. It sounded like

a man—an angry man.

"Who are you?" Hayden asked, trying to make

his voice sound deep.

I heard the strike of a match. Then a lantern

floated in front of us. Holding the lantern was a

huge man. He had black hair pulled back into a

short ponytail and he looked like those wrestlers on

TV.

"Who are you?" the man asked again. He sounded even angrier this time.

"S-sorry to disturb you, mister, but I'm looking for my uncle and grandfather," I said, trying to sound brave, but I didn't. This guy was scary.

The man held the lantern closer to me and stared at the Heartstone around my neck. "Well, you must be a Brooks," he said.

"Yes, sir. My name is Burkley Brooks. Who are you?"

"I'm Gaston, Queen Menorah's watchman. I guard the entrance of the portal. I'll be your guide each time you come here."

I remembered Grandma talking about Gaston, and I relaxed a little. He was here to help.

"Each time you come I will tell you about your task and give you a weapon," Gaston said.

"Weapon?" Cheyenne asked. "You're going to give her a weapon?"

"Hey!" I shouted.

Gaston continued. "To retrieve the next puzzle piece you'll have to defeat the sea serpent."

"The sea what?" I loved snakes, Stella especially, but I had the feeling this serpent wasn't going to be very nice. I mean, if I needed a weapon

to defeat it, that wasn't a good sign. "How am I

supposed to beat a sea serpent?"

"For one thing, if you've gotten through the

portal, then you're special," Gaston said. "And

secondly, your weapon will give you an advantage

over the serpent, but it still won't be easy."

Gaston took a seat on a large stone and placed the

lantern on the ground. "Let me tell you about the

serpent. It's been wreaking havoc under the sea for

a few weeks now, disrupting the serenity of the

ocean world. It's Queen Sedna's pet, but even she

hasn't been able to control it. The serpent

swallowed five of her loyal servants. If you can

tame the serpent and restore peace to the ocean,

then you'll earn another puzzle piece and be closer

to finding your uncle and grandfather."

"What exactly does this serpent do?" Cheyenne

asked. "I mean, besides swallow people."

"I saw a special on TV about sea serpents,"

Hayden said. "Is it true that it's long enough to

wrap around the entire world?"

"This particular serpent is only sixty feet long,"

Gaston answered.

"Only?" Cheyenne asked. "Do you have any

idea how long that is?" she whispered in my ear.

"Come with me," Gaston said. We followed him

to the back of the cave.

"You live here?" Hayden asked.

"I sure do."

There was a pile of blankets and pillows in one corner of the cave and a small burning fire next to it, but that was all. Gaston pulled something from out of a corner. It looked like a giant fork. It was taller than me.

Gaston handed it to me. "This is called a trident. When you're holding it, you can breathe under water. In order to defeat the serpent, you must strike it with this trident. When you're done come back and Queen Menorah will release your puzzle piece."

I held the trident in my hand. It was heavy and I really didn't like the idea of having to carry it around. I wondered how close I would have to be to the serpent to use it. Gaston had explained it like it was the easiest thing in the world.

"Come with me and I'll show you to your boat," Gaston ordered.

We followed him outside. An old white tugboat sat on the shore. I was sure it hadn't been there when we'd first arrived. I would have liked a nice pink and purple ship with a leopard-print flag, but the tugboat would have to do.

"Look," Hayden said pointing to the side of the boat. It said **S.S.** Brooks on the side in faded black letters.

"Wait a minute," I said. "Is that—?"

Gaston nodded. "Yes, that is your grandfather's boat. It's what you'll use to navigate your way through your challenges."

"We're nine-years-old. We don't know how to steer a boat," I said.

"I can," Hayden said, heading toward it.

I didn't feel good about this. I remembered when Hayden ruined his scooter by riding it into the large oak tree at the end of our street.

"You'll figure it out," Gaston said.

My friends looked at me. I clasped the trident tightly and swallowed my fear. "Okay, let's go."

8
SOMETHING UNEXPECTED

The small tugboat rocked back and forth as we

climbed on. I hoped it would hold up in the ocean.

"Inside the wheelhouse you'll find everything

you need to drive the boat," Gaston called.

We followed Hayden inside. There weren't any controls or buttons, just one of those old-fashioned wheels with handles on it.

"Cool, a helm!" Hayden said, grabbing the wheel.

Cheyenne and I went back on deck as the boat pulled away from the shore. Gaston waved, becoming smaller and smaller the farther out we got. It was a bumpy ride, but soon we were cruising.

While Hayden steered, Cheyenne and I watched the waves. So far, Hayden was doing a pretty good job. I leaned over the side of the boat. Mist splashed on my face—it tasted like salty soup crackers.

"Look!" Cheyenne yelled.

Three dolphins jumped out of the water. The dolphins swam closer to us. They surrounded the tugboat, bobbing up and down in the water.

"Look at that one," Cheyenne said, pointing. One of the dolphins held a bottle in its mouth. It jumped a little higher than the others.

I leaned over the edge. "I think it's trying to give it to me."

Cheyenne held me by my waist as I reached over the railing until I finally had the bottle in my hands. There was a piece of rolled up paper in it. It was a message in a bottle, like I had seen in movies.

"Who could this be from?" I asked Cheyenne.

She shrugged. "Open it and let's see."

I pulled the tan cork and removed the letter inside. The message was written on some fancy gold paper.

"Wow, look at this, Cheyenne." The letter was written in beautiful swirly letters. I wished I could write like that. Ms. Cooper would be really impressed.

She looked over my shoulder. "Read it."

I cleared my throat.

Dear Burkley,

I see that you have finally made it to Mermaid's

Lagoon. I'm happy you're here. As you know, my

sister, Queen Sedna, is holding your grandfather and

uncle hostage. She will only release them upon

completion of a number of tasks. Don't worry; I'm

making sure your family members are well taken care

of.

My sister has a problem. She had trained a

number of creatures to do horrible, evil things.

Unfortunately, the monsters are turning on her—not

even she can control them anymore. As the wearer

of the Heartstone, you have the ability to come

through the portal and battle the beasts.

I know this may seem like a lot for a young girl

to handle, but if you believe in yourself and trust

your friends, you'll be just fine. I'm sure you will be

able to complete the puzzle. Keep your eye out for

the serpent. It tends to pop up when you least

expect it. Have a safe journey.

Yours truly,

Queen Menorah.

Queen Menorah seemed like a lovely person. I

wondered if I'd get to meet her sometime. It must

be awful having a sister like Sedna. Reading that letter made me appreciate McKenna a little more. She may be annoying at times, but she wasn't evil.

"Wow," I said.

Cheyenne frowned. "So what are we supposed to do? Just sit here and wait for a sea serpent to come?"

"I don't know, Cheyenne. I've never done this before. Queen Menorah said it'll come when we least expect it." Just as I said that, dark clouds started rolling in. The wind blew stronger, making the waves rock us harder. I stepped away from the railing on the side of the boat, afraid I might fall in.

Hayden yelled something I couldn't hear. I ran into the wheelhouse. "What?"

"We're heading for some rocks," he said. Hayden looked through a pair of binoculars he had found. I took the binoculars from him and focused. Sure enough, there was a large cluster of rocks, and we were headed straight toward them!

"Hayden! Steer away! Go around!" I yelled.

He jerked the wheel to the left so roughly we both fell over. We got back on our feet, and Hayden took control of the wheel again.

Cheyenne ran inside the wheelhouse. "What are you doing? Trying to kill us?" she asked Hayden.

"It wasn't his fault," I said. "He was trying to steer us away from those rocks."

Cheyenne took the binoculars to see for herself. "Well, we're still headed for them."

"Let me see that," Hayden said, grabbing the binoculars. "Hey, I don't get it."

"Do something before we crash!" I yelled.

Hayden took the wheel and turned it in the other direction. That didn't help because the rocks moved too. I took a good look through the binoculars. Then I realized they weren't rocks at all. It was sixty feet of scary, scaly sea serpent!

9

The Sea Serpent

Hayden stopped the engine, but we still rocked

back and forth on the water. The serpent looked

like a dragon with a long snout and spikes stacked

down its back. Its skin was the color of an avocado,

and the rest of its long body coiled behind it. The

creature stared at our tugboat and then let out a

loud hissing sound, like Stella when he got mad,

times a hundred.

"What do I do?" I asked.

"You have to strike it with the trident,"

Cheyenne said.

"I know that, but how?"

The serpent ducked into the water and glided

underneath the boat then rose again on the other

side. I thought about my grandpa and uncle being in

that evil sea queen's clutches, and I got a sudden

burst of courage. I had to free them. "You guys

get in the cabin. I know what to do."

"By yourself?" Hayden asked.

"Yeah. I'm the one wearing the Heartstone. I have to defeat the serpent. It's okay. I got this," I said, trying to keep my legs from shaking. I thought about Grandma and McKenna waiting for me to bring them good news.

Hayden shook his head. "But we came here to help you, Burk."

"Yeah, that thing's huge. You need us," Cheyenne added.

I thought for a minute. Cheyenne was right. The serpent was huge, but this was my task to complete. "You guys are in charge of the boat. As soon as I spear that snake, be ready to take off."

Hayden and Cheyenne looked at each other, then Hayden nodded. "Okay, Burk, we'll be ready. Just be careful."

"I will. I promise."

Hayden and Cheyenne went into the cabin after wishing me luck. I walked to the back of the boat to face the serpent. It stared at me, flicking its long red tongue. I squeezed the trident in my hand and took a deep breath, but before I could do anything, the serpent lunged. A mouth filled with sharp teeth came my way. I jumped out of its path, and the serpent's head hit the deck of the tugboat, flipping it on end. Falling backwards, I slid down the deck and into the ocean.

Water rushed into my eyes, blinding me. I was a pretty good swimmer, but not the best. I remembered what Gaston had told me—the trident would allow me to breathe under water like a fish. I calmed down and blinked until I could see clearly. Then I took a tiny breath. No water went into my mouth or nose so I took a bigger breath. It was just like breathing out of water except bubbles came out when I exhaled.

Then I saw a dark shadow dart underneath me. The serpent rushed toward me at top speed. I didn't have much time to do anything. The serpent's body sped past, spinning me around. It swam around me in a circle, creating an underwater tornado. I spun faster and faster until I was dizzy.

Finally, the serpent stopped and disappeared from view. I saw nothing but dark blue water. Then the serpent's wide mouth came into view again. This was it. Either I had to act now, or it was game over.

Before I got Stella, Mom made me research how to handle a snake safely. Daddy bought me a book. In the book I read if your snake ever got loose to grab it gently right underneath its head, that way the snake wouldn't be able to bite you. The serpent was a lot bigger than Stella, but it was still a snake. I hoped this would work.

When the serpent was close enough to touch, I wrapped my arms around its scaly neck, just below the head. The giant snake thrashed from side to side, trying to throw me off, but I held on tight. Then I poked the pointy end of the trident into the serpent's body. That must have made it mad, because it shot through the water like a roller coaster. I held on tight, but my legs flapped around like kite tails.

Finally, the serpent slowed down enough for me to take one hand off. I raised the trident and thrust it into the back of the serpent's head. That one must have hurt, because it jerked its neck so hard, I flew off.

I did somersaults in the water, and when I stopped to look around, the serpent was coming back for me. Gaston was wrong—the trident hadn't killed the serpent. I closed my eyes and prepared to be devoured. I thought about Stella eating his mice. The serpent would swallow me whole and take twenty-four hours to digest me. My family would never see me again, and Grandpa and Uncle Charlie would be lost forever.

I waited a few seconds and when nothing happened, I opened one eye. The serpent stared at me, inches from my face. Its eyes drooped, like a baby fighting sleep. Then its body sank to the bottom of the ocean. I kicked back to the surface and took a gulp of fresh air. The water was calm and the sun shining. I spotted Hayden and Cheyenne standing on the tugboat, calling and waving to me.

I swam back to the boat and Hayden dropped the ladder so I could climb aboard. They cheered and clapped. Cheyenne wrapped a warm blanket around me, and I realized I was shivering from the cold water.

"What happened?" Hayden asked.

I told them about my near-death experience.

"Burkley you did it! So what now?" Cheyenne asked.

Hayden turned toward the wheelhouse. "I'll take the boat back to shore." Suddenly the boat rocked back and forth again, and we felt a thump from below. Everyone grabbed onto the tugboat's railing to keep from falling. Something was underneath us again.

"W-what's that?" Cheyenne asked. "I thought you took care of the serpent?"

"I did." I squinted overboard and saw them— three baby sea serpents. They were the same avocado green as their mother and each was about as long as a jump rope. Their mouths snapped as they bobbed, trying to jump into the boat.

"Awww, they're so cute," Cheyenne said.

"Let's see how cute they are when they're eating you," Hayden replied.

I shook my head. "Yeah, especially after I just knocked out their mom."

"What are you going to do, Burkley?" Cheyenne asked.

A thought popped into my head, and I snapped my fingers. "Let me try something I saw on TV." I held my fist out to the serpents.

"Burkley, are you crazy? What are you doing?" Hayden whispered.

"When you show a snake your fist it makes it look bigger and harder to bite."

The baby serpents stopped snapping at the boat but still hissed and flicked their red tongues at me.

"Your fist won't hold them back for long," Cheyenne said.

I have an idea," Hayden said. "Can't snakes be charmed by playing a flute? We need some music. Somebody sing something."

I sang my favorite song.

"Burkley-Burkley-Burkley-Burk

Burk-Burk-Burk-Burk-Burk.

Burkley-Burkley-Burkley-Burk

Burk-Burk-Burk-Burk-Burk."

Cheyenne and Hayden looked at me like I was crazy. "Don't you know any other songs?" Hayden complained.

Cheyenne pointed at the serpents. "No, look at them."

The serpents swayed back and forth to the tune of my song. Baby sea serpents must have great taste in music.

"Burk, give me that coin you found on the beach," Hayden said.

"No way. I'm saving it for my circle collection."

"Please. I need to try something."

I wasn't sure what Hayden had up his sleeve, but I fished the coin out of my sock and gave it to him. Hayden waved the coin over the baby sea serpents as they swayed back and forth to the tune of my song. Then Hayden took my coin and threw it out into the water. For a second I was angry, but then the three baby serpents turned, dove into the water, and went after the coin.

"Good thinking, Hayden. It's like fetch! Let's

get out of here while they're distracted," I said.

"All right," Hayden said, turning toward the wheelhouse. "Can we eat on the way back? Charming baby sea serpents made me hungry."

Cheyenne went inside to grab the basket, while I stood on deck as the look-out. Who knew how long a gold coin would hold the baby sea serpents' attention? If they were anything like McKenna, they'd play with it for about two minutes then get bored. Cheyenne came back out with two packages of peanut butter crackers and two bananas.

"A banana? A yellow banana?"

Cheyenne shrugged. "Sorry, Hayden packed the

food, not me."

"No thanks." I stood over the edge and watched the water closely as I ate my crackers.

I saw three small dark figures in the water. Cheyenne saw them too. "Look, I think the dolphins are coming back."

I squinted so I could see better. "No, Cheyenne. Those aren't dolphins. The sea serpents are coming back!"

"What should we do?"

Our small tugboat was no match for the baby sea serpents. They were right next to us in a matter of seconds, jumping out of the water and snapping at us again. They looked angrier this time.

"Quick, drop your crackers in!" Cheyenne yelled. We both threw our crackers into the water and watched them turn into mush, but the serpents didn't stop trying to attack us.

I shook my head and noticed the bananas. I remembered the snake's tongue that had wrapped around one at Jewel's house. "Try the bananas!" Cheyenne and I peeled our bananas, broke them in half, and tossed them into the water.

The sea serpents stopped and fought over the bananas as we moved farther and farther away from them. Soon they were out of sight. I guess yellow food isn't so bad after all. We enjoyed the ride across the peaceful ocean until the tugboat brought us back to shore. Gaston was there waiting for us.

"Well done. Not bad for a first-timer," he told me.

"Thanks, Gaston. What's going to happen to the serpent now?" I asked.

"It's in an underwater cavern, asleep where it belongs," Gaston answered. "And here is your puzzle piece."

I beamed as I held the small, darkened puzzle piece in my hand. My heart warmed, and I couldn't wait to show Grandma. Although we still had a bunch more to earn, we were one step closer to completing the puzzle.

"What now?" Hayden asked.

"You form a circle and go back home," said Gaston. "I'll be here when you come back to guide you through your next challenge."

We held hands and thought about the closet. Like before, there was a bright flash of light and then darkness. Next, the strong wind knocked us backward and we were on the water slide again. Cool water surrounded me as I slid from left to right. Down, down, we went. My stomach got that funny feeling it always has when I ride on a roller coaster. Then suddenly, the water and wind

stopped. There was another flash of light and then

it went pitch black. When we opened our eyes, we

were back in my closet surrounded by toys and

clothes. I wasn't cold and wet anymore.

"You made it!" McKenna shouted when I

opened the closet door. "Where's my souvenir?"

"Sorry, no souvenir, but we did get the puzzle

piece." I raced out of the closet.

"Grandma, Grandma, Grandma!" I screamed.

"We did it!"

Her face lit up when she saw the puzzle piece.

"There was never a doubt in my mind that you

would do it. After all, you've got Brooks blood

flowing through your veins."

Then Grandma set a tray on the table, and we

put the nine puzzle pieces together. They connected

perfectly. I realized we still had a long way to go.

Grandma gave me another squeeze. "Now go

wash up and tell me all about it over dinner."

10

JELLYFISH, SMELLYFISH

The next day I had to go to Jewel's house again

to work on our science project, but this time I had

a better idea. I hoped Jewel would go for it. We

opened our notebooks on her bedroom floor.

"I've been researching jellyfish and they're

absolutely disgusting," Jewel said. "They're not

even pretty."

"About jellyfish, I've been thinking. We should

do something else—something more interesting."

Jewel huffed and slammed her notebook shut.

"Are you crazy, Broccoli? All the research I've

been doing on those ugly things and now you want

to do something else? No way."

"First of all, stop calling me Broccoli. Second,

just hear me out. Don't you want to have the best,

most interesting project?"

"Yes," Jewel admitted.

I knew that would get her. She always had to

have the best everything.

"We should do our project on the legendary sea

serpent!" I said.

Jewel frowned. "Ewww! That's even worse than jellyfish. I hate snakes. Besides, sea serpents don't exist. That's not science."

"Sure, they exist," I insisted.

"How do you know?"

"I just do."

Jewel looked at me like I was an alien. "Broccoli Brooks, you are the biggest fibber ever! There's no such thing as a sea serpent and you've never seen one."

I didn't blame her. If I hadn't seen a sea

serpent with my own eyes, I wouldn't believe they existed either.

"Come on, Jewel. It'll be the best project ever. Everybody will love it," I said.

"Nope!"

"But no one else will have a project like ours. It'll be guaranteed to win first place. I'll even let you do all the talking."

Jewel thought about it for a second. "Fine." Then her eyes widened. "My dad's an artist. I bet he can help us make a visual aid for our project." Jewel opened her notebook. "Tell me about the sea serpent. Where does it live? What does it eat?

Where did it come from?"

"Well, the sea serpent is the pet of the Sea Queen. It lives under the ocean and it likes to eat bananas."

Jewel rolled her eyes. "Whatever, Broccoli," she muttered.

Cheyenne and Max were up first on presentation day. Their presentation was about rainbows, but Max had turned it into a report about leprechauns. He even broke into a weird leprechaun jig. Cheyenne didn't seem to appreciate that.

"Burkley and Jewel, you're up!" Ms. Cooper said. I was happy to be next. There was no way we would be worse than that.

Jewel and I went to get our project from where it rested on the back counter. The class oohed and aahed as we carried it to the front of the classroom. Jewel's dad had helped us create a sea serpent out of paper mache. We'd painted it pink and purple, even though that wasn't the color of the serpent I had seen. They were our favorite colors and we wanted the serpent to be beautiful.

At the front of the classroom, Jewel held one end of the serpent and I held the other. "This is the tale of the legendary sea serpent," Jewel began. We moved the serpent up and down so it looked like it was swimming through the water.

"Sea serpents have been around as long as man. They were even mentioned in the Bible. Sometimes they're called sea monsters or sea dragons. There have been many stories told about sea serpents, but nothing has been proven or documented." Jewel glared at me.

"Some people believe in them and some people don't," I added, "but I can tell you, they do exist."

Everyone gasped.

"Yeah, right. How do you know they exist?" yelled a boy named Buddy.

I couldn't tell them about Mermaid's Lagoon. I promised Grandma I would keep it a secret.

Jewel cleared her throat. "Anyway, sea serpents have been said to be anywhere from sixty feet long to long enough to encircle the entire earth."

"Have you really seen one, Burkley?" Hannah asked.

"I can't say that, but I know they're out there."

"Do you have a picture of one?" Elliot asked.

"No," I said sadly. Right then I wished I could take a camera through the portal, but I knew Mermaid's Lagoon had to remain a secret. I promised Grandma, and promises are forever.

Buddy frowned. "How do we know you're telling the truth?"

I shrugged. "You don't. You just have to take my word for it. I know I'm telling the truth."

The class asked more questions, wanting to know how I knew serpents really existed, but I cut them off. "I'll tell you everything you want to know about the sea serpent, but first you have to listen to the information Jewel wants to share with you." After all, she had worked hard on this project too and it was only fair that she be able to take a turn.

Jewel smiled at me for the first time ever and

read her sea serpent facts from her index cards. The class listened intently. When the project was over, we received a standing ovation on the way to our seats.

"Thank goodness that's over with," Jewel said. She seemed upset but I didn't understand why.

"I thought it turned out really well," I said.

"I hope I never have to work on a project with you again, Broccoli," Jewel said, scrunching her nose up at me.

I sighed. Back to square one.

After school I decided to try and make my own mini paper mache sea serpent. I thought it might make a nice friend for Stella.

"Burkley, check on your sister outside please," Grandma called from upstairs.

"All right," I muttered. I went in the back yard to see what she was up to.

McKenna was playing in her sandbox. "Hi, Burkley. Want to make a sand castle with me?"

"I can't right now. I'm making Stella a friend." Before I turned to go back inside, I noticed the sand rippling. "McKenna, don't move," I said in a soft voice. I didn't want to scare her.

She froze. "What? Burkley, what?" she asked, looking at me wide-eyed.

"Something moved. Something's in the sandbox."

McKenna stood up. "It's probably just a lizard or something."

I shook my head. "I don't think so."

I walked closer to the sandbox and peered inside. Sand shifted and spread itself around McKenna until it formed into eyes, nose, and a mouth. I grabbed my sister under her arms and pulled her out of the sandbox, then I screamed for Grandma.

She rushed right out. "What's the matter?"

I pointed at the face in the sand, but it was

gone. "I saw something—eyes, nose, and a mouth..."

Grandma nodded. "Get ready to go back to Mermaid's Lagoon."

"Why? What is that, Grandma?" I asked.

She put her hand on my shoulder. "The Sinister Sandman."

I squeezed Grandma's hand and nodded. I knew I'd have to go back through the Portal, but I've got Brooks blood in me, so I'll be ready. And besides, with the Heartstone around my neck and Cheyenne and Hayden by my side, nothing can beat us!

About The Author

Tiffany Nicole Smith enjoys teaching as well as writing chapter books, middle grade, and young adult fiction. She resides in Florida where she is currently working on several upcoming releases.

About Knowonder!

Knowonder is a leading publisher of engaging, daily content that drives literacy—the most important factor in a child's success.

Parents and educators use Knowonder tools and content to promote reading, creativity, and thinking skills in children from ages 0-12.

Knowonder's storybook collections and chapter books deliver original, compelling new stories every day, creating an opportunity for parents to connect to their children in ways that significantly improve their children's success.

Ultimately, Knowonder's mission is to eradicate

illiteracy and improve education success through

content that is affordable, accessible, and

effective.

Learn more at www.knowonder.com